TEDDY ROOSEVELT
COLORING BOOK

Gary Zaboly

Dover Publications, Inc.
Mineola, New York

NOTE

Theodore "Teddy" Roosevelt was the 26th President of the United States, serving from 1901 to 1909. At forty-two he was the youngest man ever to become President. He is remembered today for his many accomplishments as President, but also for his courage in the Spanish-American War as the leader of the Rough Riders and for his great love of the outdoors and the environment. Teddy Roosevelt is one of only four Presidents memorialized on Mt. Rushmore, and he remains to this day one of the most beloved public figures in American history.

Copyright

Copyright © 2012 by Dover Publications, Inc.
All rights reserved.

Bibliographical Note
Teddy Roosevelt Coloring Book is a new work, first published in 2012 by Dover Publications, Inc.

International Standard Book Number

ISBN-13: 978-0-486-47961-3
ISBN-10: 0-486-47961-7

Manufactured in the United States by Courier Corporation
47961701
www.doverpublications.com

Theodore Roosevelt, the 26th president of the United States, was born on October 27th, 1858, in New York City. During his childhood he was often sick with asthma. On one such occasion, when he was six, the funeral procession of the assassinated President Abraham Lincoln passed down Broadway right under his bedroom window. He and his older brother, Elliot (future father of Eleanor Roosevelt) were photographed looking out of the window by a cameraman on the avenue. Years later, Theodore Roosevelt and Abraham Lincoln would become two of the four American presidents sculpted on Mount Rushmore.

Theodore became fascinated by wildlife, and learned the art of taxidermy. At the age of eight he started his own private museum of stuffed animals which he called the Roosevelt Museum of Natural History.

2

Because of his frail condition and short stature, young Theodore, called "Teedie" by his parents, was often picked on by bigger boys. He gave a good accounting of himself when they fought him, but he never won.

When Theodore was an early adolescent his father encouraged him to build up both his body and his self-confidence through strenuous exercise in a gymnasium, including weight lifting. He also took up boxing lessons, and became a fearless adversary in the ring.

In his eighteenth year Theodore Roosevelt went to Harvard University. In his spare time he began writing *The Naval War of 1812*, which was eventually published in 1882.

At age twenty-two he graduated college as a member of Phi Beta Kappa, the honor society for scholastic achievement. Shortly afterwards he married Alice Hathaway Lee, whom he had met while at Harvard.

Theodore loved the outdoors so much that on his European honeymoon he climbed to the top of the 14,692-foot-high Matterhorn, one of the most difficult Alpine peaks to climb.

Back in New York, Theodore entered Columbia Law School, but after two years of study he decided to enter politics. A tough campaign earned him a seat as a state assemblyman. He became known for his unwavering determination to root out corruption in high places.

Asthma still plagued him. In 1883 he thought that a trip west might be good for his health. He went to North Dakota and hunted buffalo with a hired guide, camped under the stars at night, and bought a cattle ranch.

Not long after returning to New York, Theodore's wife and mother both died in the space of two days: the worst two days of his entire life. Grief-stricken, he left his baby girl in the care of his sister, and returned to the west. He went back to his Dakota ranch and became very skilled at raising cattle, herding, and bronc busting. On one occasion he was appointed a deputy sheriff and hunted down three outlaws who had been robbing local ranchers.

Almost three years later Roosevelt went back to New York to pick up the pieces of his shattered life. He ran for mayor, but was defeated. In December 1886 he married Edith Kermit Carow, who eventually bore him four sons and another daughter. He built a house in Oyster Bay on Long Island, and called it Sagamore Hill.

His political fortunes rose again when he served as President Benjamin Harrison's Civil Service Commissioner between 1889 and 1895, earning a reputation for his reform-minded activism. In 1895 he accepted the position as Police Commissioner of New York, and became known for his assault on vice, corruption, patronage, and blackmail, as well as his fight to clean up the city's slums.

In 1897, President William McKinley chose Roosevelt to serve as his Assistant Secretary of the Navy. On February 15th of the following year, the battleship *Maine* mysteriously blew up in Havana Harbor, and the United States declared war on Spain. Determined to take part in the campaign, Roosevelt helped form a regiment of mounted riflemen, and became its lieutenant colonel. Nicknamed the Rough Riders, the regiment's base of training was in San Antonio, Texas, home of the Alamo. Made up of cowboys, gamblers, outlaws, Ivy League athletes, miners, plainsmen, firemen, Fifth Avenue swells and even a few Native Americans, the regiment's overall commander was Colonel Leonard Wood. With the assistance of Lt. Col. Roosevelt, the Rough Riders were whipped into disciplinary shape before being transported to Cuba in June of 1898.

Unfortunately, most of the regiment's horses were not shipped out in time, and in the campaign that followed the Rough Riders had to serve as foot soldiers. But Roosevelt led his command through sweltering jungles, and planned the capture of the enemy-held town of Las Guasimas.

Roosevelt succeeded in taking Las Guasimas, and for his victory was promoted to a full colonel. A week later, the Rough Riders marched to the base of San Juan Heights, which defended the main road to the city of Santiago. Spanish guns positioned on the hills kept the regiment pinned down. Receiving orders to capture Kettle Hill, Roosevelt led his men in a charge up the grassy slope. Joined by a regiment of black soldiers—the dismounted troopers of the Ninth U.S. Cavalry—the Rough Riders took Kettle Hill and then rushed on to capture the larger Spanish entrenchments on San Juan Hill. It was a stirring victory, and it made Theodore Roosevelt a national hero.

In 1898, riding the high crest of his new popularity, Roosevelt was elected Republican Governor of New York. Once again he championed honest politics, refusing to appoint any but the most qualified to public jobs. He advocated improved labor conditions, and fought abuses by big business. He also pushed for the preservation of the state's wildlife and forests.

Against his wishes, Roosevelt won unanimously the nomination for the vice presidency of the United States under William McKinley, who was reelected president in 1900. It was an all-too brief term for both men, for McKinley was shot by an assassin on September 6, 1901. Theodore had been climbing Mount Marcy in the Adirondacks when he received word that the president was dying. Despite the rainy night, he immediately jumped into a buckboard and rode quickly down the mountainous terrain in order to reach the train station on time.

In Buffalo, New York, on September 14th, 1901, Theodore Roosevelt was sworn in as the 26th President of the United States. At age 42 he was the youngest man ever to take the oath of office as chief executive of the land. John Singer Sargent painted his official portrait.

Roosevelt was hardly the strict conservative Republican his backers had expected him to be. He espoused a new ideology called "progressivism," which included the "trust-busting" of monopolistic corporations, including banks, mines, railroads and meat-packing companies. In his own words: "My business is to see fair play among all men, capitalists or wageworkers." He coined the term "Square Deal" for his policies.

An early international challenge for Roosevelt occurred in 1902, when Germany blockaded Venezuela and threatened to land troops there because that country had refused to pay its debts. Roosevelt urged that arbitration, not violence, solve the crisis. He also reminded the German Ambassador of the Monroe Doctrine, adding that if German warships did not withdraw, American power would force them to. It worked. "Speak softly and carry a big stick," became one of his mottos.

In 1903, Panamanians rebelled against Columbia, and Roosevelt sent a battleship to assist the rebels. The United States then recognized the country's independence and purchased the rights to the isthmus of Panama. Under Roosevelt's leadership, construction began of the canal that would eventually link the Atlantic and Pacific oceans for international shipping. It was completed in 1914.

During Roosevelt's presidency, the White House and its environs became a lively, noisy place thanks to his five young children. Sometimes they would roller-skate down the hallways, or ride their pony in the rooms. Teddy often indulged their energetic play, once even pillow fighting with them minutes before he attended a state dinner. On another occasion he paused during a meeting with the Attorney General to look at Quentin's new pet snakes. But when Quentin walked on his stilts through the White House flowerbeds, Roosevelt had to draw the line.

Even the president needed time away from Washington, and he and his family would spend much of their summers at Sagamore Hill on Long Island Sound. Sometimes Teddy grew tired of secret servicemen and reporters who always seemed to crowd the estate. One day he and two of his sons sneaked down to a boat by the shoreline, and rowed across the bay to make camp on the far shore, without disturbance. Over freshly cooked steaks that evening—after a full day of exploring, swimming and chopping firewood—Teddy told the boys stories of his adventures in the Rocky Mountains.

Roosevelt's love of the outdoors was again reflected in his program of conservation and land recovery. 1902 saw passage of the Reclamation Act, which included efforts to make desert lands productive. And in 1903 the construction of the Roosevelt Dam in Arizona began and the first Wildlife Refuge was created. In 1906, Roosevelt put many historic and scientifically valuable sites under the protection of the government. By the time he left office he had doubled the number of national parks. He is shown here in Yosemite Park with naturalist John Muir in 1903.

In 1905, after Russia and Japan had been at war for more than a year, Roosevelt, during his second term in office, invited their delegates to America to confer for peace terms. The meetings helped end the Russo-Japanese War, and for his efforts Roosevelt was awarded the Nobel Peace Prize the following year.

Imperial Japan, however, continued to flex its muscles in the Pacific by increasing the size of its fleet and army. Roosevelt decided to make a symbolic statement, ordering the U. S. Navy to make a global cruise in order to display American power as well as to promote trade. Sixteen battleships, dubbed the "Great White Fleet," sailed peacefully around the world between December 1907 and February 1909.

Among the firsts for American presidents that Teddy Roosevelt could claim during his seven and a half years in office were: the first president to dine with a black man (Booker T. Washington) in the White House; the first president to appoint a Jewish-American Cabinet officer (Oscar Straus); the first president to push for pure food and drug legislation; the first president to ride in an automobile; and the first president to take a submerged ride in a submarine. He is also the only president to have had a toy named for him, the "Teddy Bear."

Although he was urged by the leaders of his party to run for another term, Theodore Roosevelt declined, feeling that one man should not hold the office too long. On March 4, 1909, William Howard Taft became the new president. Almost immediately afterwards, Roosevelt was on his way to Africa, on a combined hunting and specimen-gathering expedition he had agreed to head for the Smithsonian Institution. On one occasion a hippo attacked his canoe and almost overturned it before being shot by Roosevelt.

After his African adventure, Roosevelt went on a tour of Europe. Back in the States in the summer of 1911, he became the first former president to take a ride in an airplane. In 1912 he founded the Progressive Party, and decided to run again for president. On October 14th, in Milwaukee, an would-be-assassin wounded him with a bullet, but Roosevelt refused treatment until he had delivered his scheduled speech. That November, while Theodore was still recuperating, Woodrow Wilson won the presidential election.

In the middle of 1913, Roosevelt went on a speaking tour of South American capitals, and afterwards explored unmapped regions of the Brazilian jungle, including a river that was named the *Rio Teodoro* in his honor. When America entered the First World War, Roosevelt offered to raise a new Rough Rider regiment, but was turned down by President Wilson. His son, Quentin, however, was killed in aerial combat over France, and that loss, combined with the lingering effects of a fever he had contracted in Brazil, led to Theodore's rapid decline in health. He died at Sagamore Hill on January 6th, 1919, at the age of sixty. The man born sickly and weak had lived a life more active, inspired, and productive than most, and became one of America's greatest presidents.